20TH CENTURY DESIGN

THE 90s

THE DIGITAL AGE

For a free color catalog describing Gareth Stevens Publishing's list of high-quality books and multimedia programs, call 1-800-542-2595 (USA) or 1-800-461-9120 (Canada). Gareth Stevens Publishing's Fax: (414) 332-3567.

Library of Congress Cataloging-in-Publication Data available upon request from publisher.
Fax: (414) 332-3567 for the attention of the Publishing Records Department.

ISBN 0-8368-2710-4

This North American edition first published in 2000 by
Gareth Stevens Publishing
A World Almanac Education Group Company
330 West Olive Street, Suite 100
Milwaukee, Wisconsin 53212 USA

Original edition © 1999 by David West Children's Books. First published in Great Britain in 1999 by Heinemann Library, Halley Court, Jordan Hill, Oxford OX2 8EJ, a division of Reed Educational and Professional Publishing Limited. This U.S. edition © 2000 by Gareth Stevens, Inc. Additional end matter © 2000 by Gareth Stevens, Inc.

Picture Research: Brooks Krikler Research
Editor: Clare Oliver
Additional Research: Adam Hibbert

Gareth Stevens Senior Editor: Dorothy L. Gibbs
Gareth Stevens Series Editor: Christy Steele

Photo Credits:
Abbreviations: (t) top, (m) middle, (b) bottom, (l) left, (r) right

1st Independent (courtesy of the Kobal Collection): page 29(br).
AKG London: Cover (br), pages 18(br), 18-19, 21(b).
Courtesy of Apple Macintosh: Cover (mtl, mlt, mrt, mr), pages 3, 5(t), 7(bl), 10-11, 11(tm, bm).
Courtesy of Ron Arad Associates: Cover (ml), pages 16(t), 17(t, m), 19(all).
Ron Arad and Inflate Design Studio: page 17(b).
BMW: pages 24(m), 25(tr), 27(b).
Casio: page 8(l)
Castrol: page 25(bl).
Club Med: page 26(br).
Corbis: pages 12(br), 20-21, 22(bl), 23(r).
Division Ltd.: page 28(bl).
Freeplay: pages 26-27.
Glaxo Wellcome: Cover (tl), page 28(tl).
Lara Grylls P.R. / Becca Russel: page 16(m).
Inflate Ltd.: page 15(tl, bl).
Me Company: pages 28-29.
Mercedes-Benz: pages 4-5, 27(tr).
Milepost 92 1/2: pages 24-25.
NASA: page 28(br).
National Westminster Bank: page 8(b).
Philips: pages 9(l), 11(tr).
Redferns / M. Hutson: page 12(bl).
Renault: Cover (bl), page 25(tl).
Sharp: page 6(bl).
Solution Pictures: page 24(b).
Sony: pages 8(tr), 9(r), 10(bl).
Frank Spooner Pictures: Cover (tr), pages 4, 5(bl, br), 6(br), 6-7, 12(t), 13(tl, tr), 16(br), 18(bl), 20(m, b), 21(t, m), 22(t, m, br), 23(l), 26(bl), 27(tl), 29(bl).
Vodafone: page 7(br).
©Vogue/Condé Nast Publications Ltd. / Arthur Elgort: page 13(b).
Volkswagen: Cover (bm), page 24(t).
Zanussi: page 16(bl, bm).

Printed in Mexico

1 2 3 4 5 6 7 8 9 04 03 02 01 00

20TH CENTURY DESIGN

THE 90s

THE DIGITAL AGE

Hannah Ford

Gareth Stevens Publishing
A WORLD ALMANAC EDUCATION GROUP COMPANY

CONTENTS

Models strutted combat-style fashions on the streets of New York during the Gulf War. The war was triggered by Iraq's invasion of Kuwait in 1990. Throughout the decade, Western powers tried to remove Iraqi leader Saddam Hussein from power.

As growing congestion brought city traffic to a standstill, the world finally accepted smaller cars, such as the Smart (above) and the Ka.

A SMALLER WORLD

The 1990s opened with a recession. Throughout the economy's recovery, work and careers began to seem less important to a lot of people, and new emphasis was placed on lifestyle. Fashion reacted against the materialism of the 1980s, although any remnants of antifashion were quickly transformed by the media into the height of chic. No-name brands, such as Muji, were ultradesirable, and Alessi's tongue-in-cheek designs sold by the thousands.

Technology saw rapid changes. Computers became simpler to use — not for just whiz kids and geeks anymore — and the Internet revolutionized both communication and the marketplace. Satellite, cable, and digital TV brought the world closer to almost everyone, starting with round-the-clock satellite news coverage of the Gulf War, at the beginning of the decade, and ending with troubles in the Balkans, civil wars in Africa, and border disputes in Asia.

The Italian firm Alessi brought fun, friendly designs into people's homes.

Working from home, or telecommuting, became a reality in the 1990s. The colorful iMac was aimed at the home market.

5

Virtual stars appeared in the 1990s — and were easier to control than human ones!

The Millennium Dome in London was built to usher in the 21st century and to serve as a showcase for new technologies.

DIGITAL DECADE

Digital technology was the gold mine of the 1990s. Amazing new products appeared every year, and by the end of the decade, it had become a part of everyday life. Most households had personal computers connected to the World Wide Web, and microchips ran everything from TVs to toasters.

DIGITAL DAWN

Although digital technology was available in the 1960s, only governments, universities, and large businesses took advantage of its benefits. As computers became easier to use, however, and microchips became faster, smaller, and more reliable, "digital" became more and more commonplace. Information is now almost instantly accessible and can easily be exchanged just by swapping computer files, and many household objects are now sophisticated, yet simple to use, electronic devices.

The Nikon E2 digital camera, introduced in March 1996, transferred photographs directly to a computer, eliminating expensive film processing.

Widespread ownership of video players in the 1990s created a big market for easily operated video cameras. This Sharp Viewcam has a flat screen mounted independently of the lens, allowing the filmmaker to hold the camera away from the eye.

Digital technology united television and computing. Digital broadcasts freed up airspace for new channels, and the Internet could be accessed from television sets, such as the Philips Web TV (1996).

As digital devices came into wider use, making computers more user-friendly became vital. The Apple Newton pocket-size computer *(below)* lets users write by hand. A special pen presses together two transparent, conductive, metal wiring grids, creating tiny electrical charges. The computer "feels" the pattern of the charges and figures out what was written. Charges in the grid turn tiny LCDs black, making the writing visible — in digital ink!

pen (stylus)

conductive metal sheet covered with a protective layer

conductive metal sheet

miniature LCD layer

information to processor

gel

THE END OF VIDEO?

The first digital storage and retrieval system, the Digital Versatile Disc (DVD), was marketed in 1998. One DVD machine could do most of the jobs previously done by separate machines — video players, CD players, and game consoles. Digital technology gave DVDs the advantage over these older machines. Skipping to a favorite part of a movie without having to wind a tape backward or forward was now possible. DVDs will also last much longer than magnetic tape; they do not become fuzzy as they get older.

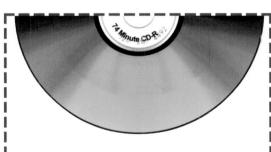

DIGITAL vs. ANALOG

Digital systems use On and Off (1 and 0) coding to carry and process information. Analog systems use changes in the strength of a signal to reproduce information. In the 1990s, digital systems replaced most analog ones because digital is quicker, cheaper, and more reliable and portable. Some people, however, believe that analog provides better quality.

Handwritten notes can be faxed from a pocket-size computer, such as the Apple Newton (1993), via a mobile phone, or they can be taken home and downloaded onto a word processor.

7

MICRO GADGETS

The mass production of microchips spawned a new generation of micro gadgets — a weather station that fit on a wristwatch, a navigator that could be tucked into a pocket, and a whole collection of top 1,000 pop tunes you could hold in the palm of your hand!

SONY

PYXIS

GLOBAL POSITIONING SYSTEM

The Sony Pyxis handheld Global Positioning System (GPS) was the perfect navigator for explorers and hikers. By comparing tiny delays from three satellite signals, it calculated its position to within a few yards (meters).

MICRO STYLING

As more people were able to afford sophisticated electronic gadgets, the demand for smaller and more stylish designs grew. Mobile phones shrank from the size and weight of a briefcase to slimline pocket handsets that were easily taken everywhere. Styles progressed from ugly black bricks to shiny contours in a rainbow of colors.

The Casio Alti-Thermo mountain watch (1993)

OFF-ROAD COMPUTING

Inexpensive microchips made entirely new products possible. The Casio Alti-Thermo wristwatch, designed for mountain climbers and skiers, contained two sensors that read air pressure and temperature. From changes in air pressure, the watch's microchip calculated height above sea level.

Mondex (1990) made it possible to carry a bank around in your pocket. Mondex cards store electronic "cash" on a microchip that can be read with a key fob, allowing cardholders to make transactions that otherwise require a trip to the bank.

£48.69

STORE=WALLET
PRESS KEY:

ON/OFF
LOCK/UNLOCK
SELECT
TRANSFER
CLEAR/CANCEL
BALANCE
STATEMENT
CURRENCY
ENTER/YES
SET/CANCEL CODE
CHANGE CODE
WALLET
CARD
LOCK AVAILABLE

8

FIGHTING FOR THE FUTURE

Manufacturers combined imagination and digital technology to create new markets — by inventing the GPS, for example. Sometimes, however, new products clashed, and companies had to fight for a position in the digital future.

In their search for the smallest of everything, manufacturers occasionally missed the mark. Not many people wanted to watch television while they were jogging.

The Philips Digital Compact Cassette Player (1992) was meant to replace tapes, but clever design did not always ensure success in the market.

OUT WITH THE OLD

By the 1990s, digital recordings on compact discs had conquered the music industry. Tape recorders now seemed too bulky and slow, and two possible replacements emerged: MiniDisc and DCC, a digital tape. As these two formats battled it out, the future arrived, in 1998 — MP3. With MP3, music could be downloaded from the Internet onto a microchip and played at CD-quality for hours.

THE MAGIC OF MINIDISCS

Typically, CDs are made by burning holes into metal foil with a laser, which makes a recording that can never be changed. To make its MiniDisc (1992) re-recordable, Sony had to invent a new system. MiniDisc recording heads combine two very different technologies. First, a laser beam softens the metal in a tiny spot. Then, a magnetic head swipes the hot spot, leaving a pattern of magnetized metal. When a special polarized light is bounced off the surface, the magnetic spots make the beam change very slightly. The change is just strong enough for the disc player to decode as music.

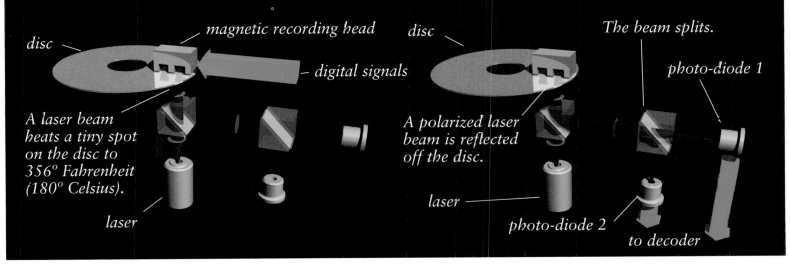

disc

magnetic recording head

disc

The beam splits.

— *digital signals*

photo-diode 1

A laser beam heats a tiny spot on the disc to 356° Fahrenheit (180° Celsius).

A polarized laser beam is reflected off the disc.

laser

laser

photo-diode 2

to decoder

COOL COMPUTERS

Before the 1990s, computers were rarely seen outside of big offices, factories, and universities, but wider use and lower cost soon made them desirable for home use, too. Sometimes home computers were used for working — but they were also great for playing games!

OFFICE BORE

Outside of cost, the problem with computers for home use was that they looked like ugly square lumps. Since the early days of office machinery, computers had been made in army-regulation beige because the U.S. army was one of the computer world's best customers. Since people now wanted computers at home, designers began to rethink styling. Apple led the way in the late 1990s with a new line of colorful computers for home or office. Using one of these computers felt more like playing than ever before!

Nintendo's Game Boy enjoyed a revival in the late 1990s, when it was rebuilt with trendy new plastics.

10

Sony's PlayStation (1996) brought more computer power to video games than it took to put a man on the Moon.

POCKET PETS

In trying to make computers more friendly, designers discovered that they could give them personality, too. A worldwide craze started in 1997 for Bandai's Tamagotchi, an egg-shaped toy containing a virtual pet on a microchip. If the pet was not cared for properly, it would become a little monster — or die!

Tamagotchi was the size of a key ring.

Apple designed iMacs (1998) with translucent, candy-colored plastic casings to make them fun for the home.

Apple made the eMate (1997) tough enough to handle rough treatment from school-children.

Home computers such as this interactive Philips system can teach basic math and reading skills.

WIRED WORLD

The most important innovation of the computer revolution was the World Wide Web. At first, the Internet was hard to understand. Until 1993, it was used mainly by scientists. Then, the release of a new and simpler computer code led to the World Wide Web, and the Internet boom began. By 1998, the Web was an important part of the world economy, and "surfing" it for art, music, and games, as well as for information, was a cool new hobby.

GETTING CONNECTED

Some home computer systems had scanners, digital cameras, and CD drives for loading music and pictures that could be sent over a modem to a Web site for other people to access from anywhere in the world. Downloaded files could be saved to a hard drive, printed out, played over speakers, or recorded onto a removable disk or a CD.

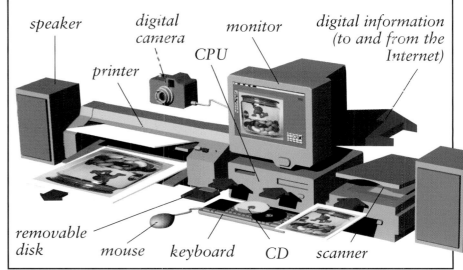

speaker   digital camera   monitor   digital information (to and from the Internet)

CPU

printer

removable disk   mouse   keyboard   CD   scanner

FASHION

Reacting against the showy power suits of the 1980s, postmodern designers of the 1990s plundered the past. Besides reviving styles of the 1940s, 1950s, 1960s, and 1970s, they also looked to popular culture for fresh ideas. Sports and dance were rich sources of inspiration.

SHOCK TREATMENTS

Famous in the 1970s and 1980s as the "mother of punk," British designer Vivienne Westwood (*b*.1941) continued to create fashions with shock value in the 1990s. Westwood cleverly mixed visual motifs of the past and present. Her Vive la Cocotte collection in 1995, for example, revived 18th-century ball gowns, and the Anglomania collection of 1993 combined denim streetwear with oriental motifs.

12

Increasingly, in the 1990s, fashion became an expression of beliefs and a way to present challenging ideas.

Vivienne Westwood's outrageous creations, such as this ball gown from her 1995 collection, reclaimed historical styles that once imprisoned women.

WESTWOOD'S LEGACY

Designers of the 1990s updated punk fashions of the 1970s. Androgynous cyberpunks looked like they had stepped off the set of a science-fiction film, dressing in leather, plastic, rubber, and even metal fabrics, with accessories made from "found" objects.

Metal strainers made perfect goggles for this punk ensemble!

During the 1980s, clothes and materials developed for sports led to a new trend in mainstream fashion. New synthetics, such as Tencel and Polartec, joined DuPont's Lycra, and windproof, waterproof, breathable, Gore-Tex was no longer worn only by skiers and snowboarders. Nike covered their state-of-the-art running shoes with it, and U.S. designer Ralph Lauren (*b*.1939) used it for his RLX label, introduced in 1999.

Windproof: the outer shell deflects wind.

Gore-Tex keeps out the elements but allows perspiration to evaporate.

outer shell

Waterproof: each pore is 20,000 times smaller than a raindrop.

Breathable: micropores allow body moisture to escape.

inner shell

French couturier Jean-Paul Gaultier often wore skirts, challenging the stereotypes of male and female fashion.

French designer Jean-Paul Gaultier (*b*.1952) was also out to shock people. He championed the "underwear as outerwear" look, designing glitzy, jewel-encrusted corsets for pop singer Madonna's "Blonde Ambition" tour.

ANTIFASHION

Casual clothes, particularly stretchy leggings and comfortable athletic shoes, slowly became wardrobe staples, making Nike, Adidas, and Reebok household names. Streetwise brands, such as Firetrap and Diesel, used high-tech fabrics for their laid-back fashions, and, before long, top designers were copying them.

Sportswear went high-fashion with these Chanel athletic shoes (1997). The V-neck shirt is by Escada Sport.

13

FUN AND STYLE AT HOME

GioStyle's Flori collection includes a juicer and a multi-purpose canister, both in candy-colored plastic.

Departing from the modernist ideal of "form follows function," postmodern designers considered an object's form first — sometimes at the expense of its function.

USEFUL vs. PLAYFUL

The postmodernist response to modernist style was often humorous. One of the ways postmodern designers related the form of a product to its function was almost cartoonlike — a colander shaped like lettuce leaves, for example. Many of Alessi's household items, which included Coccodandy (an egg boiler with a hen-shaped handle) and plastic spice jars with models of their contents (nutmeg, chili, basil, and so on) on their lids, were playful designs.

Philippe Starck's Juicy Salif lemon squeezer (1990) was beautifully designed and sold extremely well. A glass placed inside the juicer's long, stylish legs collected the juice.

ON DISPLAY

Objects that once were barely noticed, such as toilet brushes and lemon squeezers, now were designed for display. In fact, the Juicy Salif lemon squeezer, with its rocket-launcher silhouette, was too tall to fit into most cupboards!

In a witty interpretation of "form follows function," this colander resembles the salad greens it was designed to drain!

HOLLOW PLASTIC

Some of the latest plastic objects looked good enough to eat — and were made in an Easter-egg fashion. (1) A drop of liquid plastic was poured into half of a mold. (2) The other half of the mold enclosed the plastic. (3) The closed mold was gently rocked to coat the entire inside surface with a thin layer of liquid plastic.

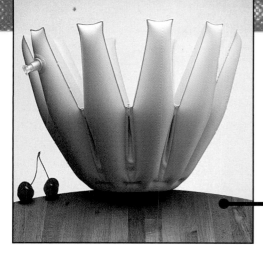

The British firm Inflate used PVC for its playful products, such as this inflatable fruit bowl.

NEO-POP

Many 1990s designers looked back at the pop art of the 1960s for inspiration, but replaced sleek metal with bright, kindergarten colors. Low-cost, versatile plastic became more popular than ever. Inflate (*f.1995*) used dip-molded PVC to create inflatable household items, ranging from chairs to fruit bowls! Modern "hard" plastics were translucent, matte-finished, and, actually, "soft" to the touch.

At home in kitchen or office, Inflate's Digital Grass was a letter rack — that could also hold toast!

(4) The molded plastic object came out completely smooth, with no seams or rough edges.

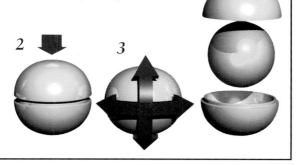

1 2 3 4

The Little Devil bottle opener (1994) was designed by Biagio Cisotti for Alessi.

ALESSI

In 1993, Italian manufacturer Alessi introduced its Family Follows Fiction (FFF) line. The items were made using a mixture of polyamide plastic and stainless steel. The "family" included Gino Zucchino (a sugar sifter), Carlo (a bottle cap), Gianni (a glass storage jar), and Mary (a plastic cookie bin). Alessi gave the items friendly names to encourage a relationship between product and consumer. Bright colors gave the FFF line toylike appeal, and items were expensive and exclusive to prove that *plastic* didn't necessarily mean "cheap."

The full name for Alessi's humorous storage jar was "Gianni, a little man holding on tight!"

15

The Anna G corkscrew (1994), designed by Alessandro Mendini, started a whole range of Anna G products.

Instead of sharp steel blades, Alessi's Folpo (1998) whisk had colorful legs that looked like octopus tentacles. Folpo is Venetian slang for "octopus."

CURVY FORMS

Like product designers of the 1990s, furniture makers also reverted to the soft, curvy forms of the 1960s. Chairs, tables, and shelves had organic shapes, but they were built with man-made materials such as plastic, glass, and steel. Unnatural colors boldly emphasized that these pieces were not organic at all.

Ron Arad combined ultramodern materials (see-through plastic on a tubular aluminum frame) to create a curvy effect for his Fantastic Plastic Elastic chair (1997).

This simple but elegant glass chair by Becca Russel (1999) is four sheets of bent glass bolted together.

COOL FRIENDS

While major appliances were usually box-shaped and had a white enamel finish, some 1990s designers decided to give them organic forms. The Swedish company Zanussi gave its products soft, rounded feet and friendly names, instead of numbers. A washing machine prototype named Zoe (1999) could decide which wash cycle to run.

Zoe

Oz refrigerator (1998)

Designers can play tricks with texture. Curvy objects might look soft and squishy, but Starck's inviting chaise lounge is made of hard, polished metal.

METAL'S SHELF LIFE

Israeli-born Ron Arad (*b.*1951) was trained as an architect, but he began to design furniture in the 1980s for his London shop, One-Off. His early pieces were constructed mainly from metal and concrete. Arad also built shelving systems using pieces of industrial scaffolding. Bringing scaffolding into a home was unusual, but very practical; the shelf heights could be adjusted as shelving needs changed.

REINVENTING THE WHEEL

Arad was known for his unconventional forms. His storage systems included the Bookworm bookcase (1992) — one long piece of metal bent into a surreal shape — and the RTW bookcase (1996), which was a technological triumph. Equipped with a free-spinning outer wheel, the RTW could be rolled anywhere in the room. The shelves were locked inside the wheel and always stayed right side up — even when the bookcase was moving!

Arad's Bookworm was shaped like a long, wriggly worm. Metal bookends, which looked like books, were riveted in place.

Thanks to RTW's revolutionary design, books always stayed level.

Do-It-Yourself Design

A collaboration between Ron Arad and the British design company Inflate led to the Memo chair — a unique piece of tailor-made furniture. The chair could be molded to perfectly fit the contour of a person's body. A person simply sat in the chair, then used a vacuum cleaner to suck out the excess air. The fun came from having a hand in creating the final product.

Any vacuum cleaner could mold the Memo, but the bagless Dyson Dual Cyclone was the only one as unconventional as the chair!

INTERIORS

Sophisticated consumers demanded stylish surroundings for their leisure. To attract classy customers, hotels, restaurants, and night clubs hired star designers to give their interiors a makeover.

MIX AND MATCH

French designer Philippe Starck styled interiors in every major city of the world. Starck's inventiveness stemmed from his ability to mix unusual materials and textures. For the Asahi Company's Super Dry Hall in Tokyo (1989), he created a romantic look with gold tassels and padded walls in lush, maroon velvet. He used padded walls again for the Felix Discotheque in Hong Kong (1993), along with textured glass tables that were lit from the inside and rose from the floor like sculptures.

18

Starck's interior design for the Peninsula Hotel included the eerie lighting and lime green walls of the space-age Felix Discotheque on the twenty-ninth floor.

Philippe Starck (b.1949)

STARCK FACTS

Although trained as an architect, Philippe Starck won worldwide fame with designs that include toothbrushes, kettles, chairs, and complete buildings. Much of his work is called "biomorphic," meaning his objects imitate the appearance of living things.

Starck styled every last detail in the Peninsula Hotel — even the organic, twisted metal bathroom faucets.

INSPIRED INTERIOR

High-tech style, which revived the use of raw, industrial materials such as metal and concrete, began in the 1980s. This style was embodied in the work of Ron Arad — but Arad softened the look.

Arad's interior for the London restaurant Belgo Noord (1994) included his signature curves, along with black and neutral, metal and wood mixtures.

Arad's most influential interior was the new Tel Aviv Opera House. Many designers of the 1990s copied its style. The Opera House had clean, white walls, completely free of pictures and ornaments — but the design was far from stark. Although the walls were bare, their curves created organic holes that invited a clever play of soft light, providing a perfect backdrop for the glittering bronze staircase.

The centerpiece of the foyer in the Tel Aviv Opera House (1988) was a stunning staircase of beaten bronze.

Arad converted an abandoned warehouse for his studio and furniture showroom (1991). The office space had a skin of PVC stretched over a steel shell.

ARCHITECTURE

Postmodern architects played with more new designs and materials than ever before.

The Guggenheim Museum in Bilbao, Spain, was completed in 1997.

COMPLEX BUILDINGS

American Frank Gehry (*b*.1929) was one of the most imaginative architects of the postmodern age. His designs broke all the rules. He even built a restaurant shaped like a fish! Rather than creating huge monoliths, Gehry composed clusters of smaller units to develop organic, sprouting structures. Gehry's designs for the Guggenheim Museum in Bilbao, Spain, and the Frederick R. Weisman Art Museum in Minneapolis demonstrate his complex style.

20

Kansai International Airport (1995)

FEAT OF ENGINEERING

With land at a premium in Japan, the architect for the new airport headed out to sea. Italian Renzo Piano (*b*.1937) built Kansai International Airport on a man-made island in Osaka Bay, linked to the mainland by a bridge that is 2 miles (3 kilometers) long. A high-tech roof of undulating glass and steel makes the airport's architecture as impressive as its engineering. The sea cushions the building during earthquakes.

BUILT-IN TECHNOLOGY

British architect Terry Farrell (*b*.1940) came up with a suitably forbidding architectural style for the new headquarters of the British secret service. Vauxhall Cross (1993) is a perfectly symmetrical structure, decorated with alarming spikes. Its concrete walls have a built-in mesh that stops electromagnetic information from passing into or out of the building.

The exterior of Vauxhall Cross is deliberately inscrutable.

Shining titanium walls with a bricklike texture emphasize the curves of the Bilbao Guggenheim, creating distorted reflections of the museum's industrial location and the nearby sea.

The Getty Center, in Los Angeles, with its pavilions, gardens, cafes, restaurants, and galleries, is like a miniature city dedicated to art and culture. The Center, designed by Richard Meier (b.1934), was completed in 1997.

The zigzag structure of the Jewish Museum has been compared to a bolt of lightning. The walls are covered with zinc.

MEMORIAL MUSEUM

Completed in 1999, the Jewish Museum in Berlin, Germany, is architecture with a powerful message. Its architect, Daniel Libeskind (b.1946), planned the museum around a central space — a void. The emptiness is a reminder of Berlin's missing Jews, who either fled Nazi Germany or died in concentration camps. This imposing structure also demonstrates that what an architect leaves out can be as important as what an architect puts in.

MIGHTY MONUMENTS

The 20th century ended with a flurry of building. The new structures celebrated the present and looked forward to the future with the same sense of optimism as postwar skyscrapers such as the Seagram Building.

TECHNOLOGY ON DISPLAY

The industrial look was a style of architecture that featured technology. British architect Richard Rogers (*b.*1933), known for his futuristic approach in designing the high-tech Pompidou Center in Paris, in 1977, and collaborating with Renzo Piano on the Lloyd's Building in London, in 1986, showed the struts, girders, and other supports architects usually want to hide. Constructed for the year 2000, Rogers's beautiful Millennium Dome at Greenwich, London, proudly displayed how it was built, too. Twelve steel masts painted an eye-catching orange rose 328 feet (100 m) into the sky to support a fabric roof of Teflon-coated glass fiber.

Hans Hollein's (b.1934) Haas Haus in Vienna (1990) mixed stone veneer and glass to reflect both the city's history and its future. The interior (top) has a stunning, celestial ceiling.

The fabric roof of London's Millennium Dome has a life span of about fifty years. Many critics disapproved of the dome because this "temporary" building (left and above) cost £750 million.

22

TOWERING GIANT

When the economies of Southeast Asia exploded during the 1980s, those countries raced to build prestigious skyscrapers. Argentine-born architect Cesar Pelli (b.1926) designed a uniquely Malayan building, which, at eighty-eight stories high, broke the Sears Tower's twenty-two-year record as the world's tallest office building. Completed in autumn 1997, Pelli's Petronas Towers is 1,476 feet (450 m) high. Its symmetrical exterior, topped with two pinnacles, each 241 feet (73.5 m) high, was influenced by the intricate, geometric patterns of Islamic art. Sixteen columns at the base of each tower helped the building reach its record-breaking height.

The unique sky bridge that links the twin pinnacles of Petronas Towers at the forty-second story gives the building additional support and makes it look like a gateway. Petronas Towers is, in fact, the entrance to the "Golden Triangle" business district of Kuala Lumpur.

Cesar Pelli designed Britain's tallest building, Canary Wharf Tower, in 1991. This fifty-story, 800-foot (244-m) obelisk was the first skyscraper to be covered with stainless steel — 16,000 pieces of it!

DESIGNS ON WHEELS

While the focus of transportation design is primarily on safety and performance, a trend toward "friendly" designs also emerged in the late 1990s.

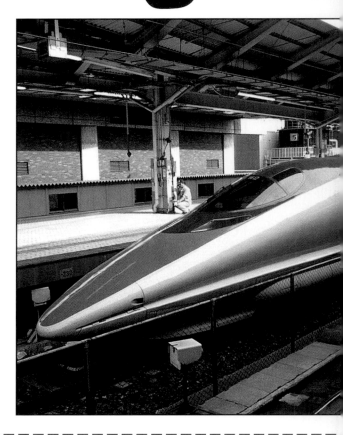

An updated Volkswagen Beetle came out in 1998.

TOYS FOR GROWN-UPS

To avoid urban traffic congestion, some city-dwellers of the 1990s turned to bikes and scooters. New bike designs had rounded styling that appealed to both men and women. Toylike microcars, such as Ford's curvy Ka, appeared, too, and, in 1998, Volkswagen updated the classic VW Beetle. The new Beetle kept the lovable, facelike front of the original but, overall, had a more stream-lined appearance and was easier to handle.

Bike or car? BMW blurred the boundaries with the weather-proof C1. The C1's tubular aluminum frame had crumple zones to protect a rider in a crash.

Some of the newest cars offer a built-in navigator. This satellite-linked, electronic route planner helps a driver find the quickest routes and avoid traffic jams.

THE QUEST FOR SPEED

In October 1997, British driver Andy Green set a 1-mile (1.6-km) land speed record in the Nevada Desert when he drove his car *Thrust SSC* faster than the speed of sound. *Thrust SSC* is powered by two aircraft-style Rolls-Royce jet engines that generate 50,000 pounds (22,680 kilograms) of thrust. It was the first car in history to break the sound barrier.

With more and more cars on the roads, especially in cities, parking spaces become harder to find. Renault's *Matra Zoom*, the prototype for an energy-efficient electric microcar, solves the parking problem. This tiny compact can make itself smaller for parking by tucking its back wheels under its body!

Cruising at 186 miles (300 km) per hour, the Nozomi *(left) is the fastest of the Japanese bullet trains. The* Hikari *(right) is slightly slower.*

Computer-aided design (CAD) gave designers of the 1990s more freedom to try out their ideas. By computer, they could create a model of a vehicle, based on their specifications, and test that vehicle's performance without the cost of building a prototype.

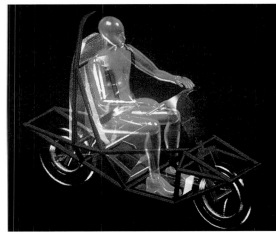

A CAD-produced image of BMW's C1.

TOP TRAINS

The *Nozomi 500*, one of the Japanese bullet trains known as *shinkansen*, holds the record for the fastest travel time by train. Its super-sharp nose cuts through the air at an average speed of 163 miles (262 km) per hour. The fastest European train is the French *Train à grand vitesse* (TGV). Although its average travel speed of 158 miles (254 km) per hour is slower than the *Nozomi 500*, the TGV *Atlantique* hit a record-breaking top speed of 320 miles (515 km) per hour in 1990. The Anglo-French *Eurostar* can travel 187 miles (300 km) per hour.

Thrust SSC *topped 761 miles (1,225 km) per hour.*

The Eurostar *(1994)*

GOING GREEN

Environmental concerns raised in the 1980s trickled into the trends of the 1990s as designers started to use recycled and recyclable materials and to create products that were kind to the environment and did not use too much of the world's precious energy resources.

RECYCLED CLOTHING

Green concerns have led to the development of eco-friendly fabrics. Tencel is a strong, stretchy fabric made out of wood pulp that is gathered from sustainable forests. The synthetic fleece Polartec is made from recycled plastic bottles.

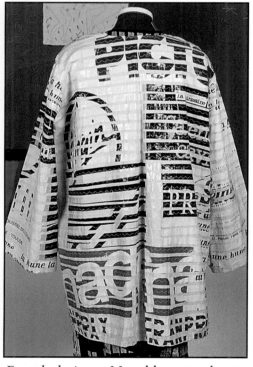

French designer Myrold creates haute couture out of used plastic bags.

WINDUP MERCHANDISE

British inventor Trevor Baylis (*b.*1937) invented the windup radio in 1993 with the developing nations of the world in mind. People in remote parts of Africa were not receiving safety information because they could not afford batteries for a radio. Baylis's Freeplay radio had three possible power sources: a spring for winding it up, a rechargeable battery, and solar panels. Baylis also invented a windup flashlight.

Boats went back to sail power to cut costs and save fuel. With less fuel to carry, ship designs could be more streamlined.

26

Vehicles emit millions of tons of exhaust gases each year. A green solution to city pollution was the pedicab, which does not burn fuel at all. Based on the Japanese rickshaw, the pedicab ran on pedal power.

The Smart car was a collaboration between Mercedes-Benz and Swatch. At only 8 feet (2.5 m) long, this energy-efficient two-seater was the perfect vehicle for space-conscious city-dwellers.

To prove that sensible technology can look good, too, Freeplay products came in fashionably colored plastics — solid yellow or black, as well as transparent blue, red, or green.

CLEANING UP THE AIR

Cars are one of the chief causes of air pollution. As fuel burns in a car's engine, the car's exhaust emits harmful gases. Measures to combat emissions pollution included the introduction of catalytic converters, unleaded gasoline, and the use of alternative fuels, such as electricity, solar power, and biogas. In the 1990s, smaller, more fuel-efficient vehicles became acceptable to consumers. Some people even left their cars at home and used public transportation or pedal-powered bicycles and pedicabs.

A LOAD OF RUBBISH

In the 1990s, after decades of being a throwaway culture, the public learned to recycle. People sorted their bottles and newspapers into different bins. Products, such as laundry detergent, became available in refill sizes to minimize wasteful packaging. Newspapers switched to being printed on recycled paper. New fabrics appeared — created from yesterday's garbage! Even car makers took part. The BMW 3 series demonstrated eco-awareness with parts of its bodywork (shown in green) molded from recycled plastics, and almost all of its remaining body parts (shown in blue) made from recyclable plastics.

The BMW 3 series

VIRTUALLY REAL

Huge leaps in computer power during the 1990s led to the creation of very lifelike, computer-generated models of the world. Instead of staring at a flat picture on a computer screen, it was now possible to put on a virtual reality (VR) suit and climb right inside the picture.

Pop stars and advertisers used computers to make their products more interesting. In her music video for Hunter *(1997), Björk was morphed into an animal by computer.*

Scientists could use virtual reality to test ideas. This young scientist is building new molecules by hand.

LIKE REALITY — ONLY BETTER!

Although first used mainly for video games, virtual reality has all kinds of uses. Nuclear testing, for example, can be modeled on a computer, instead of actually being done.

THROUGH THE LOOKING GLASS

Virtual reality links your body to a computer by means of sensors that detect movement and calculate your new position, including your new view of the space. You feel that you are "in" the picture the computer is creating. Advanced versions of VR include little machines in the gloves and boots that resist when you press them. If you reach out to grab a virtual object, the glove actively pushes against your fingers to let you "touch" the object, rather than letting your hand pass through it.

movement sensor

movement sensor

monitor

computer

Since virtual designs are easily adjusted, designers can achieve perfection.

For the cover of Björk's album, Homogenic *(1997), Me Company designers used state-of-the-art computers to reshape the singer, creating extraordinary eyes, hair, fingernails, and clothing.*

For countries with emissions pollution problems, VR offered the prospect of virtual offices. Instead of driving polluting vehicles to work, people could stay home, put on a headset, and telecommute.

VIRTUAL DANGER

There was also a scary side to virtual reality. In the film, *The Matrix* (1999), machines used virtual reality to control people.

Kyoko Date (1996), the first virtual superstar, was a computer-generated 16-year-old pop star, with a huge following in Japan. She was designed by HoriPro to be every teenager's dream date.

GENERATION NEXT

Virtual reality technology might have many benefits — and pitfalls. The 1992 film *The Lawnmower Man* explored what might happen if VR was used to help people overcome learning difficulties. Although the film ended badly, it made people realize that new generations growing up with VR technology would see and feel things that adults before them had never experienced. Would the gap between adults and children grow as more of a young person's life was spent in cyberspace? Would children learn faster and then grow smarter than their parents?

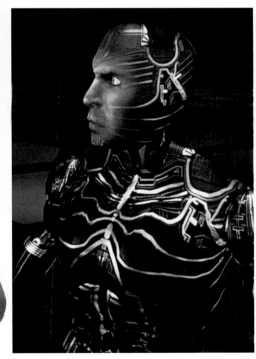

The Lawnmower Man *(1992)*

· TIME LINE ·

	DESIGN	WORLD EVENTS	TECHNOLOGY	FAMOUS PEOPLE	ART & MEDIA
1990	•*Philippe Starck: Juicy Salif (for Alessi)* •*Gaultier designs costumes for Madonna* •*Hollein: Haas Haus*	•*Gulf War breaks out as Iraq invades Kuwait*	•*Hubble Space Telescope launched* •*TGV Atlantique hits 320 miles (515 km) per hour*	•*Nelson Mandela freed in South Africa* •*Artist Keith Haring dies*	•*The Simpsons* •*Bassomatic: Set the Controls for the Heart of the Bass* •*Jeunet/Caro: Delicatessen*
1991	•*Ralph Erskine: the London Ark* •*Pelli: Canary Wharf Tower*	•*Breakup of USSR*	•*Dyson's bagless vacuum cleaner wins design prize*	•*Yeltzin is Russian leader* •*Aung San Suu Kyi wins Nobel Peace Prize* •*Calvin Klein signs model Kate Moss for $2 million*	•*Jostein Gaarder: Sophie's World* •*Douglas Coupland: Generation X* •*Katsuhiro Otomo: Akira*
1992	•*Gehry: Powerplay armchair*	•*Australia drops oath of loyalty to Queen of England*	•*Philips: Digital Compact Cassette (DCC)*	•*Warhol's Marilyn x 100 sells for $3.4 million*	•*Koons: Puppy* •*Brian Eno: Nerve Net* •*Prince: Love Symbol Album* •*Jungle music is born*
1993	•*Starck: Peninsula Hotel* •*Alessi: Family Follows Fiction* •*Farrell: Vauxhall Cross*	•*PLO and Israel sign peace agreement*	•*Apple: Newton* •*Casio: Alti-Thermo watch*	•*U.S.: Bill Clinton elected president*	•*Spielberg: Jurassic Park* •*Björk: Debut* •*E. Annie Proulx: The Shipping News* •*Tim Burton: The Nightmare before Christmas*
1994	•*Alessi: Anna G corkscrew*	•*South Africa: Mandela is first black president* •*Civil war in Rwanda*	•*Channel Tunnel completed* •*Genetically modified tomatoes first sold*	•*Kurt Cobain commits suicide*	•*Tarantino: Pulp Fiction* •*Damien Hirst: Away from the Flock* •*Helen Chadwick: effluvia* •*Irvine Welsh: Trainspotting*
1995	•*Inflate founded* •*Westwood: Vive la Cocotte collection* •*Piano: Kansai International Airport*	•*U.S.: Terrorist bomb blast in Oklahoma City* •*Kobe earthquake* •*Tokyo: Nerve gas attacks by Aum Shinrikyo cult*	•*Baylis: Freeplay windup radio*	•*Israel: Prime Minister Yitzak Rabin assassinated* •*O.J. Simpson acquitted in murder trial*	•*The Prodigy: Music for the Jilted Generation* •*Seamus Heaney wins Nobel Prize* •*Christo wraps the Reichstag* •*Tank Girl*
1996	•*Arad: RTW bookcase* •*Nikon E2 digital camera* •*Philips Web TV*	•*"Mad Cow" disease: bans on British beef*	•*Sony: PlayStation* •*UK: Sea Wraith (stealth ship prototype)*	•*Francois Mitterand dies* •*Artist Helen Chadwick dies* •*Tomb Raider Lara Croft is born*	•*Disney: Toy Story* •*Spice Girls: Spice* •*John Pawson: Minimum* •*Orange Prize for Fiction launched*
1997	•*Arad: Fantastic Plastic Elastic chair* •*Gehry: Bilbao Guggenheim* •*Meier: Getty Center* •*Pelli: Petronas Towers*	•*UK returns Hong Kong to China* •*Roswell report denies alien encounter* •*UK: Blair named prime minister*	•*Bandai: Tamagotchi* •*Dolly the Sheep cloned* •*Sojourner Rover on Mars* •*Thrust SSC breaks sound barrier* •*Apple: eMate*	•*IBM's Deep Blue beats Kasparov at chess* •*Princess Diana dies* •*Versace shot* •*Ousland crosses Antarctica alone*	•*Alex Garland: The Beach* •*Elton John remasters Candle in the Wind in response to the death of Diana, Princess of Wales*
1998	•*Apple: iMac* •*"New" VW Beetle* •*Alessi: Folpo*	•*South Africa: Truth and Reconciliation Report* •*Birth of the euro currency*	•*Construction begins on International Space Station* •*First vertical-drop theme park ride: Oblivion* •*Digital Versatile Disc (DVD)*	•*Frank Sinatra dies* •*Japanese director Akira Kurosawa dies* •*Linda McCartney dies*	•*Anish Kapoor exhibition* •*Talvin Singh: ok* •*Ted Hughes: Birthday Letters*
1999	•*Smart car* •*Rogers: Millennium Dome* •*Libeskind: Jewish Museum*	•*NATO air strikes on Yugoslavia* •*India and Pakistan: Nuclear testing crisis*	•*Zanussi: Zoe washing machine, Oz refrigerator, and Teo oven*	•*Madonna becomes face of Max Factor* •*Prince Edward marries Sophie Rhys-Jones*	•*Lucas: Star Wars: Episode 1 – The Phantom Menace* •*Philip Glass: Dracula* •*Pokemon*

GLOSSARY

androgynous: having both male and female qualities or suitable for both males and females.

biogas: a methane and carbon dioxide fuel mixture made from decomposing organic waste.

eco-friendly: designed to support and sustain natural elements and the environment.

ensemble: a complete outfit of coordinated clothing and accessories.

haute couture: high fashion; trend-setting fashions by well-known and exclusive designers.

Internet: a huge electronic network that links computers throughout the world.

monolith: a massive block or column of stone or a massive structure built in the form of a single block or column and often made of stone.

morphed: changed in form; transformed.

obelisk: a tall, four-sided, monolithic column or pillar that usually tapers as it rises and has a pyramid-shaped top.

organic: found in nature or designed to resemble a living thing from nature.

prototype: an original model of a product, which is subsequently copied to mass-produce the product.

PVC: the abbreviation for "polyvinyl chloride," which is a synthetic plastic material.

sustainable: capable of being used and replaced without permanently damaging or depleting the supply.

telecommute: to work from home using an electronic link or network to a central office at a distant site.

World Wide Web: a network, or "web," of information contained on computers that can be accessed over the Internet.

MORE BOOKS TO READ

The 80s & 90s: Power Dressing to Sportswear. 20th Century Fashion (series). Clare Lomas (Gareth Stevens)

Alessi. Alberto Alessi (Konemann)

Beetlemania: The Story of the Car That Captured the Hearts of Millions. Kate McLeod (Smithmark)

Cesar Pelli. Architects — Artists Who Build (series). David Anger (Capstone Press)

Communicating on the Internet. The Internet Library (series). Art Wolinsky (Enslow)

Digital Revolution. Twentieth Century Inventions (series). Stephen Hoare (Raintree/Steck-Vaughn)

Guggenheim Bilbao Museoa. Opus: Architecture in Individual Presentations #32. Frank O. Gehry (Edition Axel Menges)

Philippe Starck: Subverchic Design. Cutting Edge (series). Fay Sweet (Watson-Guptill Publications)

Virtual Reality: Experiencing Illusion. New Century Technology (series). Christopher W. Baker (Millbrook Press)

WEB SITES

BayGen: about Trevor Baylis, the inventor of the windup technology. *www.windupradio.com/trevor.htm*

Beyond the Wall 26.36°: Daniel Libeskind. *www.nai.nl/libeskind*

Design: An Introduction. *www.iswonline.com/centdesign.html*

Zanussi: Design & Innovation. *www.zanussi.com/index1.html*

Due to the dynamic nature of the Internet, some web sites stay current longer than others. To find additional web sites, use a reliable search engine with one or more of the following keywords: *Alessi, Apple computers, Ron Arad, digital technology, DVD, Gaultier, Gehry, Gore-Tex, Internet, microchip, minidisc, Philippe Starck, virtual reality,* and *Zanussi.*

INDEX